UNSHAKABLE

7 Proven 3-Minute Mindset Drills for Young Athletes to Master Mental Toughness, Crush Goals, and Forge Exceptional Character

FROM: _______________

TO: _______________

DATE: _______________

NOTE: _______________

Disclaimer and Legal Notice

TABLE OF CONTENTS

YOU CAN'T

PRAISE

Terrence M., 8th Grader and AAU Basketball Player

I already had *Called to Be a Champion* and it changed how I see myself as an athlete. When I got *UNSHAKABLE*, it felt like the **daily training plan to lock everything in**. I do not read much, but the **3-minute drills are so short I actually do them every day before school in my room**. The character drill hit me hardest. I used to **talk trash after every play and thought that was confidence**. Now I realize **real toughness is staying locked in when things go wrong, not when things go right**.

My family cannot afford trainers or camps like other kids on my team, but **these drills cost nothing and still work**. The goal drill helped me **break my free throw percentage into daily targets instead of just hoping I would improve**. The biggest change is in games. I used to **shut down in the fourth quarter when we were losing**. Now I get louder. **Leader loud, not trash talk loud.** My AAU coach pulled me aside and said I look like a **completely different player in tight situations**.

Between both books, I feel like I finally have a **plan for becoming the player God is building me to be**. I am **more confident, more focused, and more of a leader** than I have ever been.

Marcus T., Father of a 14-Year-Old Soccer Player

My son wanted to quit after getting pulled at halftime while his replacement scored twice. He did all seven drills from *UNSHAKABLE* that night. The mental toughness drill changed everything. He used to **spiral after mistakes and mentally check out**. Now he **resets in seconds**. His coach noticed before I did.

What surprised me most is how it showed up off the field. He has become **kinder and more respectful at home**. We now talk through one drill on the drive to practice, and it has become **the best part of my week**. If your kid struggles with confidence or shuts down after mistakes, **this book does the heavy lifting without feeling like a lecture**.

Brianna K., Varsity Volleyball Player

The goal drill changed everything for me. I went from **74 percent to 89 percent serving accuracy in one month** because I finally had **daily targets instead of goals that lived in my head**. The mental toughness drill lets me **reset in about ten seconds after an error instead of replaying it for rotations**. Teammates started asking why I stay calm, and I just handed them the book. Three minutes a night feels like **sharpening a blade**. I am **becoming someone I respect on and off the court**.

Rebecca D., Mother of a 15-Year-Old Swimmer

My daughter hit a **mental wall last year**. Plateaued times and tears before meets. *UNSHAKABLE* gave her a reset. She now uses the mental toughness drill between laps and her **splits are consistent again**. She does **one 3-minute drill every morning**. The biggest change is her **confidence and character**. She is **calmer, kinder, and believes in herself again**.

Coach Vanessa R., Head Varsity Girls Basketball Coach

After 14 years coaching, the hardest part has never been X's and O's. It is **helping teenage girls believe they belong**. *UNSHAKABLE* does what I have tried to do in pregame talks for a decade. We run one **3-minute drill before practice**. The mental reset is now part of our pregame routine, and my point guard said she feels like she has **already handled adversity before tip-off**.

The goal drill gave my players **measurable targets instead of vague improvement wishes**. One sophomore improved her **defensive rotations in two weeks**. The character drill changed our culture. **Leadership, encouragement, accountability**. I am ordering copies for every freshman.

Pastor Mike S., Youth Pastor and Team Chaplain

Athletes give you about four minutes of attention before they tune out. *UNSHAKABLE* fits perfectly because each drill is **three minutes**. I used the mental toughness drill with a football team before a playoff game and you could feel the **focus shift**. One player later told me it made him realize he had been a **terrible teammate,** and he apologized to others on his own. That is **real heart change**.

PRE-GAME

January 8th, 2012. NFL Playoffs. Denver Broncos vs. Pittsburgh Steelers. Overtime.

The entire sports world had spent the whole season saying **Tim Tebow couldn't play quarterback**. Not "he needs work." Not "he's developing." They said he flat out could not do it. ESPN ran entire segments breaking down why his throwing motion was broken. Analysts laughed on camera. Draft experts called him a project that would never finish. Social media was ruthless. The jokes never stopped.

And now here he was. **Overtime. One play could end the season.** Seventy five million people watching on TV. Every single critic with their arms folded waiting for him to prove them right.

Tebow dropped back to pass. The Steelers sent pressure. He stepped up in the pocket, calm as Sunday morning, and launched the ball downfield to Demaryius Thomas. Thomas caught it in stride, broke a tackle, and sprinted into the end zone.

Eighty yards. Touchdown. Game over. Broncos win.

The stadium erupted. Tim Tebow dropped to one knee on the turf, right there in the middle of the chaos, and prayed. Not for the cameras. Not for a highlight clip. He prayed because that's who he was before the play, during the play, and after the play. The same God he talked to in the quiet of his hotel room that morning was the same God he thanked with seventy five million people watching.

And here's the part that will mess with your head. **Tebow didn't throw that touchdown because the critics stopped doubting him.** They never stopped. He threw it because he had already seen it. He had spent weeks visualizing game winning drives with so much detail he could feel the laces on the football. He had trained his mind just as hard as he trained his arm. And when the moment came that would have made most guys freeze up, his brain said, **"Oh, I've been here before. I know exactly what to do."**

That's not luck. That's not just talent. **That's mental toughness backed by faith.** And it's exactly what this book is going to teach you.

But before we go any further, I need to ask you something real.

Have you ever had a game where your body showed up but your brain didn't?

You know what I'm talking about. You've done that exact move a thousand times in practice. But the lights came on, the gym got loud, your coach was staring, and suddenly your hands forgot how to work. Your legs felt like concrete. Your confidence vanished.

And the worst part wasn't even the mistake. **The worst part was the car ride home.** Sitting there quiet. Replaying everything. Wondering what happened. Wondering if you're actually as good as you thought you were.

Or maybe it's not even game day. Maybe it's the tryout you're terrified about. The position battle you don't think you can win. The teammate who seems to get all the attention while you grind in silence. The coach who doesn't see you. The voice in your head that whispers **"you're not enough"** and gets a little louder every week.

Yeah. I know that feeling. **And every elite athlete who ever lived knew it too. Every single one.**

Michael Jordan was cut from his high school basketball team. Cut. The guy most people call the greatest ever was told he wasn't good enough to make the squad. He went home, closed his bedroom door, and cried. But here's what he said later: **"I can accept failure. Everyone fails at something. But I can't accept not trying."**

Serena Williams lost big matches and faced doubt her entire career. Her response? **"If anything, losing makes me even more motivated."**

Thomas Edison failed over ten thousand times trying to invent the light bulb. Ten thousand. You know what he said about it? **"I have not failed. I've just found 10,000 ways that won't work."** And then he found the one way that changed the entire world. You're reading this under electric light right now because one person refused to let failure be the end of the story.

Steve Jobs dropped out of college, built a computer that barely sold, and got kicked out of his own company. The company HE created. Then he came back and turned Apple into the first trillion dollar company in human history. Oprah Winfrey was told she was "unfit for television" and demoted from her job as a news reporter. Today she's worth over three billion dollars and has influenced more people than almost anyone alive. Michael Jordan missed more shots than nearly anyone who's ever played the game. And Kareem Abdul-Jabbar, the all time leading scorer in NBA history? He also holds the record for the most missed shots ever.

The person who succeeded the most also failed the most. That's not a coincidence. That's the formula.

Failure is not the opposite of success. **Failure is the road to success.** And every young athlete who learns to get back up after getting knocked down, every single time, is building something inside themselves that trophies can't measure and rankings can't capture.

So here's the real question.

Why do two athletes with the same talent end up in completely different places?

One makes the team, the other gets cut. One hits the clutch shot, the other freezes. One bounces back from a bad game, the other spirals for weeks. Same hours of practice. Same drills. Same coaches. Totally different results.

The answer is always between the ears and deep in the spirit. Mental toughness is the difference. And right now, almost nobody is training it.

Think about your week. You've got practice multiple times for your body. Coaches run plays, drill footwork, push conditioning. But where's the training plan for your mind? What's the drill for when anxiety hits before a big game? What's the play when confidence crashes after a rough quarter? What do you do when that voice inside you says **"you're going to choke"** and it's getting louder by the second?

Most young athletes have zero answer. **It's not their fault. Nobody handed them one.**

Until now.

This book gives you **seven three minute mental toughness drills**. Each one is backed by real brain science, proven by real Christian athletes, and anchored in real Scripture. Every chapter tells you the story of an athlete who faced something brutal, shows you the exact drill that changed the game for them, explains why it works according to science, and gives you the verse that holds it all together.

Three minutes per drill. That's shorter than one scroll session on your phone. And if you stack all seven, that's **21 minutes a day to train the one thing that actually decides whether you win or lose.**

You're going to meet Steph Curry, Kevin Durant, Tim Tebow, Serena Williams, Manny Pacquiao, Usain Bolt, and Giannis Antetokounmpo. Every one of them was doubted. Every one of them failed. And every one of them built a mind and a faith so strong that the doubts and the failures became fuel instead of finish lines.

But let me be real with you about something before we start.

This book is not for everybody.

If you want a shortcut that makes you mentally elite by Friday, close this book right now. Mental toughness is not a microwave meal. **It's a slow cook.** It takes daily reps. It takes showing up when you don't feel like it. It takes being honest with yourself about where you're weak. If you want easy, this isn't it. But...

> » if you're TIRED of playing below what
> you know you're capable of

> » If you're done letting nerves rob your
> performance when it matters most

» If you want to stop being the kid everybody
says "has potential" and start being the kid
who actually shows up and dominates

» If you want to train the part of you that really runs the show.

Keep reading. Every word in this book was written for you.

Now let me say something about the people sitting in the bleachers pulling for you, or maybe sitting in the car reading this alongside you right now.

Your parents are your greatest teammates.

I know, I know. Sometimes they get on your nerves harder than a bad ref. Sometimes they say stuff after a game that makes you want to put your headphones on and disappear. But here's what's true: when everybody else moves on, when the coach stops calling, when the teammates go their separate ways, when the crowd forgets your name, **your family is still there.**

They're the ones driving you to six AM workouts. They're the ones paying for gear and camps and gas. They're the ones who lose sleep worrying about your future. They're your real ride or dies. The people who will ride with you through every win and every ugly loss, or die trying.

And yeah, they'll get it wrong sometimes. They'll say the wrong thing after a tough game. They'll push when you want space or give space when you need a push. That's part of it. Nobody has a perfect playbook for this. But the greats understood something early: **the most successful young athletes in the world don't do this alone.**

They let their parents help them. They listen even when it's annoying. They trust that twenty or thirty extra years of life experience is worth paying attention to.

Dell Curry helped Steph figure it out. Richard Williams wrote the entire blueprint for Venus and Serena before they could walk. Manny Pacquiao's mother sacrificed everything so he could chase a dream that seemed impossible.

Behind every great young athlete is a family that refused to quit

on them.

Let your family in on this journey. Read this book with them if you can. It'll mean more than you think.

Here's how to use what you're about to read. Go in order. Don't skip chapters. Each one builds on the one before it like a real training program. Skipping is like skipping leg day. It always shows up eventually. After each chapter, practice that drill for at least a week before adding the next. Let it become part of you.

And seriously, share this book with someone. A teammate, a training partner, a friend who competes. Do the drills together. Hold each other accountable. **Champions don't build themselves in isolation.**

One last thing.

Every athlete in this book had a moment where the world looked them in the face and said **"you are not enough."** Too small, too poor, too slow, too unlikely. And every single one of them had a relationship with God that carried them through the season where nothing made sense yet.

This book is built on a belief that I hold deeper than anything: **God did not create you to be average.** He put that fire in your chest, that love for competition, that hunger to be great for a reason. And when you combine the mental tools in these chapters with the faith that the God of the universe is walking beside you through every single rep, game, and setback, something shifts inside you that no opponent, no critic, and no bad game can take away.

You picked up this book. Most kids your age wouldn't. That already tells me something about who you are.

Now let's go prove it.

BONUSES

» **TRAIN YOUR MIND LIKE YOUR BODY**: master verses anytime with 50 fun, game-ready flashcards on

» **INSTANT CONFIDENCE**: hints + scripture help you remember what each verse means, fast.

» **PARENTS INCLUDED**: 20 bonus cards to coach, quiz, and grow together

» **SCAN THIS QR CODE AND GET ACCESS TODAY!**

Stop navigating the high-pressure, toxic sports and school culture alone.

Join a our community of Christian parents dedicated to building rooted reens who are even stronger in their faith.

What's Inside the Community:

» Safe Community: Connect with parents who value character over the scoreboard.

» Use the map to connect to other Christian parents close to you who also bought our books and joined.

» Get all of our next books sent to you for free as an advanced reviewer.

» Custom Worship Song: A professional anthem featuring your teens name & scripture of your choice ($250 Value!)

» Recruiting & Scholarship Kit: Clear steps to the next level without the stress.

» More bonuses and materials will be added!

Scan the QR code to Join us.

1

IDENTITY DECISION – STEPH CURRY

Every superhero has an origin story.

Spider-Man got bit by a radioactive spider. Batman lost his parents in an alley. Miles Morales got zapped and suddenly could turn invisible and shoot venom blasts from his hands. Cool, right? But here's the thing nobody talks about. The superpowers didn't make them heroes. The decision did. Miles had to decide: "I'm Spider-Man now." Before the suit. Before the training. Before anyone believed him. He looked in the mirror and made the call.

That's not just a movie moment. That's a real-life cheat code. And one of the greatest basketball players who ever lived used it before the whole world, on national TV, with "I can do all things" written right there on his sneakers.

Let's talk about Steph Curry.

Picture this: Chase Center, Golden State Warriors home court. Eighteen thousand fans are going absolutely nuts. Steph, the point guard who's basically the size of your cool older cousin, pulls up from way beyond the three-point line. Like, "bro, that's basically half court" deep. A defender is draped all over him. Doesn't matter. The ball rolls off his fingertips with that buttery high arc, spinning under the arena lights like it's got GPS locked in.

Swish.

Record number 2,974. The most three-pointers in NBA history. A record people said would never be broken. His teammates tackle him. His dad, Dell, is crying courtside. His mom, Sonya, looks like she just watched a miracle, because honestly? She did. And Steph drops to his knees on the hardwood, points straight up to heaven, and whispers two words:

Thank You.

If you saw that clip on YouTube or TikTok, you probably thought, "Man, Steph's just built different." And you'd be right. But not for the reason you think.

Rewind. Go back before the fame, the rings, the Under Armour deal, all of it. High school Steph Curry was six feet tall, 160 pounds. That's basically a stretched-out pool noodle with a jumper. College scouts looked at him and said, "Nah." Virginia Tech, where his own dad played, said, "Pass." Big-time programs ghosted him like a bad text thread. One coach literally said he'd "get eaten alive" at the next level.

Ouch.

So where did Steph end up? Davidson College. A school so tiny you'd drive right past it and not even notice. Nobody gets recruited from Davidson. Nobody becomes an NBA legend from Davidson.

Except Steph did. And here's the plot twist. The decision happened before the results showed up.

See, Steph didn't grow up in a regular household. He grew up in a house where faith was the Wi-Fi. It was always connected, running in the background of everything. His parents, Dell and Sonya Curry, didn't just take their kids to church on Sundays and call it good. They prayed together. They studied Scripture together. And when every college rejection hit, the message in that household didn't change: "Your size is not your limit, Steph. God's plan is."

So Steph made a decision. Not a wish. Not a "hopefully one day." A straight-up, no-turning-back, write-it-on-my-shoes DECISION. He wrote "I can do all things," Philippians 4:13, right on his kicks and walked onto every court like the verdict was already in. Like God had already stamped APPROVED on his future and he was just waiting for the rest of the world to catch up.

That's not cockiness. That's faith with sneakers on.

And that decision, made in a tiny dorm room with zero proof it would work, changed the entire sport of basketball. Forever.

Now let me hit you with a second origin story, because this one is wild.

Halfway across the world, in the Philippines, a kid named Manny Pacquiao was living in a situation that makes Steph's look like a vacation. We're talking real poverty. Like, "can't afford rice tonight" poverty. At fourteen years old, Manny left home with basically nothing, moved to Manila, and slept on cardboard on the street. Fourteen! Most of us at fourteen are arguing about what to watch on Netflix. This kid was trying to survive.

But here's where it gets superhero-level crazy. Manny decided, on that cardboard, with an empty stomach, with absolutely zero evidence, that he would become a world boxing champion.

Not "I hope so." Not "maybe if I'm lucky." He decided like it was already done.

And what happened? Manny Pacquiao became a world champion in eight different weight divisions. EIGHT. That had literally never been done in the history of boxing. He's now a born-again Christian, an ordained pastor, and one of the most generous athletes on earth. He once said something so simple it hits like a truck: "God gave me this talent. My job is to not waste it."

Manny didn't wait for life to get easier before he decided who he was. He decided FIRST. Then life rearranged itself around that decision.

Okay. Time out. Let's bring this home to YOU.

Because I know what you might be thinking: "That's Steph Curry and Manny Pacquiao. They're legends. I'm just... me."

And honestly? That's exactly what Steph and Manny thought at one point too. Steph was just a skinny kid from Charlotte that colleges didn't want. Manny was just a hungry kid sleeping on cardboard. They weren't born legends. They became legends the moment they decided who they were.

So here's the real question, and I need you to not just read this, I need you to let it hit:

Have you decided who you are?

Not who your coach says you are after one bad game. Not who that kid in the group chat says you are. Not who the algorithm shows you that you should be. Who have you decided you are?

Because here's the cheat code that every mentally tough athlete figures out sooner or later: you don't wait to feel confident and then decide. You decide first, and the confidence follows. It's like in a video game. You don't get the power-up after you've already beaten the boss. You pick it up before the boss fight, and it gives you what you need to win.

Look at Joshua 1:9 again. God didn't say, "Hey Joshua, wait until you feel brave, and then I'll send you into battle." Nope. He said BE courageous. That's a command. That's God saying, "I'm not asking you to feel it first. I'm telling you to decide it. I've got the rest."

God's basically saying: "You decide. I'll back you up. Let's go."

And the wild part? You don't have to make that decision alone. When you declare who you are every morning, the God of the entire universe is already walking with you. "For the Lord your God will be with you wherever you go." That's not a suggestion. That's a promise. From the same God who split oceans and raised the dead. He's on your team. For real.

So maybe right now you're the kid who got cut. The one sitting on the bench. The one who missed the shot when everyone was watching. The one whose body doesn't look like the starter's. Cool. That's just the loading screen. That's not the game. The game starts the moment you decide who you are and whose you are, and you stop letting the world write your story for you.

Steph made that decision in a dorm room in Davidson. Manny made it on a piece of cardboard in Manila. You can make it right here, right now, wherever you're reading this.

And once you make it? Like, really make it?

Game. Changed.

The Science Behind the Decision

Okay let's get nerdy for a second, in a cool way.

When you speak a decision out loud (not just think it, actually say it), you activate two major power systems in your brain. First: your prefrontal cortex. That's basically your brain's mission control. It handles decisions, planning, and focus. Second: your reticular activating system, or RAS. Think of your RAS as your brain's search engine. You know how when you learn a new word, suddenly you hear it everywhere? That's your RAS. When you declare "I am disciplined" out loud every morning, your RAS starts filtering your whole day to find opportunities to be disciplined. And it ignores the junk that doesn't match.

Scientists call this self-affirmation theory (Cohen & Sherman, 2014), and the research is legit: athletes who speak identity-based affirmations before competition have lower stress hormones and perform better under pressure. And James Clear, who wrote Atomic Habits, found that saying "I am a hard worker" changes behavior way faster than saying "I want to win." Why? Because your brain always acts in line with the story you tell it about yourself. New story equals new actions. It's basically reprogramming your character in real life.

Three minutes. Every morning. Out loud. That's all it takes to start rewiring your brain.

Prayer

Lord, help me decide who I am in You before the world tries to decide for me. Give me courage to speak it and faith to walk in it. Amen.

Reflection: The Steph Curry and Manny Pacquiao Lesson

Steph and Manny didn't wait for the world to give them permission. They decided who they were, rooted in faith and not in circumstances, and their lives followed that decision.

Ask yourself: What's one thing I've been "hoping" for instead of deciding, and what if I just decided today?

Mindset Drill: The Decision Declaration (3 Minutes, Every Morning)

Think of this as your daily power-up before the day tries to boss you around.

» Step 1: Grab a notebook, index card, or even your phone's notes app. This is your Declaration Card.

» Step 2: Write one sentence starting with "I am." Not "I hope." Not "I wanna be." You ARE.

> "I am the hardest worker in every room."

> "I am someone who never quits."

> "I am clutch under pressure."

» Step 3: Write one Scripture underneath it. If you're stuck, start with Philippians 4:13 or Joshua 1:9. You'll find more as you go.

» Step 4: Stand up. Say both lines out loud. Not whispering into your pillow. OUT LOUD. Like you're telling the universe what's about to happen. Let your voice hit the walls.

» Step 5: Do this every morning BEFORE you check your phone. Before Instagram, before texts, before the world tells you who you are, YOU tell the world.

Pro Tip: Stick your Declaration Card on your bathroom mirror, inside your locker, or on the back of your phone case. Steph wrote his on his shoes. Manny carried his in his heart. You pick your spot, just make sure you see it every single day. Repetition isn't boring. Repetition is how belief goes from your head to your bones.

Mental toughness starts with a decision, not a feeling. Steph Curry decided he was elite when every major college told him he was too small. He wrote Philippians 4:13 on his shoes and rewrote basketball history. Manny Pacquiao decided he'd become a champion while sleeping on cardboard at fourteen, then became an eight-division world champion and a pastor. Your identity must be set before game day, or game day sets it for you. Speak your declaration out loud every morning. Decision plus faith equals unstoppable confidence.

If You Want to Dive Deeper

Check out The Purpose Driven Life by Rick Warren. It's GREAT, and Michael Phelps said it literally helped him get through one of the darkest chapters of his life. Real talk.

QUICK TIMEOUT

Your feedback is a true blessing!

If this book has encouraged you or helped you feel less alone, would you leave a quick review?

Even one sentence makes a huge difference and takes just a minute. As a small author, your feedback not only lifts my heart... it also helps other children of God find the support and hope they need.

Thank you for being part of this journey!

Scan this QR code with your phone to go to the review page and find this book.

Or

Go to your orders, find the book and click

"Write a product review"

Thank you <3

2

STUDY THE GOATS – KEVIN DURANT

"Before honor comes humility." — Proverbs 15:33

The arena is deafening. Oracle Arena, Oakland, California. Game 3, NBA Finals, 2017. Kevin Durant catches the ball at the top of the key, and every human in that building knows what's about to happen. He rises up. All six feet, ten inches of pure, fluid, impossible length. The defender is right there. Hand in his face. Doesn't matter. KD's release point is so high it might as well be in outer space. The ball floats off his fingertips with a silky rotation that looks more like art than athletics.

Swish. Dagger. Championship sealed.

KD drops 39 points that night. Wins Finals MVP. The kid who was once told he was too skinny to survive in the league is now standing on the biggest stage in basketball, confetti falling like snow, holding a trophy that weighs almost as much as he did at the combine. And what does he do? He grabs the mic, tears running down his face, and thanks God. Thanks his mom. Thanks the journey.

But here's the part most people missed. The part that made all of this possible. The part that happened years before the confetti, before the MVP trophy, before any of it.

Kevin Durant was obsessed with homework. Not school homework. Film homework.

Rewind to young KD. Lanky. Awkward. So skinny that at the NBA Draft Combine, he couldn't bench press 185 pounds. Not even once. Scouts literally wrote in their reports that he was "too weak to survive physical NBA play." Picture that for a second. You're about to enter the most elite basketball league on the planet, and grown men in suits are writing you off because your arms look like breadsticks.

Most kids would have panicked. Hit the weight room 24/7. Tried to become something they're not. But KD did something way smarter. Something most people don't have the humility to do.

He studied the greats.

While other young players were trying to invent their own style and go viral, KD was sitting in dark rooms watching film. Frame by frame. He studied Dirk Nowitzki's one-legged fadeaway like it was a cheat code. He broke down Kobe Bryant's footwork like a scientist examining DNA. He watched Michael Jordan's mid-range game on repeat until his eyes burned. He analyzed how Larry Bird used angles to create shots that shouldn't exist.

And here's the thing that separates KD from players who just "watch highlights." He didn't study these guys to copy them. He studied them to absorb them. He downloaded the best pieces of every great scorer in history, combined them with his own God-given 6'10" frame and ridiculous wingspan, and created something the basketball world had never seen before. A player who could score from literally anywhere, in any way, against anyone.

Two-time NBA champion. MVP. Four-time scoring champion. One of the most unstoppable offensive players to ever breathe.

And he has Proverbs 15:33 tattooed on his body. "Before honor comes humility." Right there on his skin. Permanent ink. That tattoo tells you everything you need to know about how Kevin Durant thinks. He made himself low enough to learn. And that's exactly what made him great.

Now let me take you to a completely different world. No hardwood floors. No sneakers. Just a canvas ring, heavy leather gloves, and a giant named Wladimir Klitschko who had been destroying every heavyweight on the planet for over a decade.

Enter Tyson Fury. Six foot nine. 270 pounds. A boxer from a Traveller family in England who most experts thought had zero chance. Klitschko was a machine. Clinical. Precise. He'd knocked out champion after champion with the same robotic jab and terrifying right hand. Nobody could crack the code.

But Fury? Fury didn't just train his body. He trained his eyes.

For months before the fight, Fury studied hundreds of rounds of Klitschko's footage. He watched the jab timing. The clinch patterns. The distance management. The way Klitschko shifted his weight before throwing the right hand. Fury didn't just glance at highlights on YouTube. He sat down, locked in, and engraved every pattern into his brain like a student cramming for the biggest exam of his life.

Fight night. Dusseldorf, Germany. Klitschko's home turf. 55,000 fans screaming for the champion. And Tyson Fury walked into that ring and outboxed the most dominant heavyweight of the modern era. Made him look confused. Made him look human. Won a unanimous decision and shocked the entire world.

After the fight, Fury pointed straight up. He said: "I studied my enemy, I prepared my body, and I trusted the Lord."

Two athletes. Two sports. Same formula. Humble yourself. Study the best. Download the blueprint. Then go perform.

So let me ask you something real. When was the last time you actually sat down and STUDIED someone better than you?

Not scrolled past their highlights while eating cereal. Not double-tapped a dunk compilation on Instagram. Actually studied. Paused. Rewound. Watched their feet. Their hips. Their eyes. Their positioning. The stuff that doesn't make the highlight reel but wins the actual game.

Because here's what most young athletes get wrong. They think studying someone else means admitting they're not good enough. Like watching film of a pro is some kind of weakness. "I don't need to copy anyone. I'm my own player."

Nah. That's not confidence. That's pride. And pride is a performance killer dressed up in a cool outfit.

KD didn't think he was too talented to study Dirk. Fury didn't think he was too tough to study Klitschko. Kobe Bryant built his ENTIRE career on studying Michael Jordan so closely that you can pull up side-by-side videos and the moves are identical. Move for move. Step for step. Kobe never hid it either. He said, "I stole all of MJ's moves and I'm proud of it."

Humility isn't thinking less of yourself. It's thinking of yourself less, long enough to learn from someone who's further ahead.

And here's where this hits YOUR life. Right now. Today.

You've got a phone in your pocket that gives you access to every great athlete who ever lived. Every game. Every move. Every technique. For free. KD had to track down VHS tapes and DVD footage. You can pull up full NBA games from 1998 on YouTube in three seconds. You have more access to greatness than any generation of athletes in human history.

But what are you actually watching?

Because your brain doesn't know the difference between a real pro performing under real pressure and some kid filming trick shots in his backyard with a ring light and 47 takes. Your subconscious absorbs whatever you feed it. If you feed it polished, pressure-tested excellence, that's what it downloads. If you feed it sloppy, edited-for-likes content, that's what it installs. And then you wonder why your game feels off.

Philippians 4:8 says, "Whatever is true, whatever is noble, whatever is right, whatever is pure, whatever is lovely, whatever is admirable, if anything is excellent or praiseworthy, think about such things." Run everything you watch through that filter. Is it true performance or manufactured content? Is it excellent or just entertaining? Guard what goes into your eyes the same way you guard the ball. Because what your eyes absorb, your body will eventually produce.

The greats you study become your invisible coaches. The content you scroll becomes your invisible influence. Choose wisely. And choose humbly.

Because the moment you're willing to sit down, shut up, and learn from someone ahead of you? That's not weakness. That's the exact moment your game starts to level up.

KD did it with a tattoo of Proverbs on his body and a stack of game film. Fury did it with months of footage and faith in God's plan. And you can do it with three focused minutes and a decision to be a student before you try to be a star.

The Science Behind Engraving (Why Watching Actually Builds Skill)

Here's where it gets wild. Your brain has something called mirror neurons, discovered by researcher Giacomo Rizzolatti in 1996. These neurons fire both when you perform an action AND when you watch someone else perform it. That means watching a pro execute a crossover, a jab, or a serve literally activates the same brain circuits you'd use to do it yourself. Your brain is practicing while your body sits still.

But here's the catch. Casual, distracted watching doesn't trigger mirror neurons the same way. You need focused, intentional observation for the download to work. This is why researcher Daniel Coyle, in The Little Book of Talent, describes what he calls the "engraving technique." When athletes repeatedly watch elite performers with locked-in attention, their brains build high-definition mental blueprints. Those blueprints become the template the body follows during practice.

Tennis coach Timothy Gallwey proved this on national TV. He took a complete beginner, had her do nothing but watch him demonstrate skills for twenty minutes, and she showed dramatic improvement before she ever hit a ball. The blueprint was installed. The body just ran the program.

Three minutes of focused watching. That's all it takes to start building your blueprint.

Prayer

Lord, give me the humility to learn from those ahead of me, the focus to study with purpose, and the faith to trust that You are building something great in me. Amen.

KD and Fury didn't rely on raw talent alone. They humbled themselves, studied the greats before them, and combined those lessons with their own God-given gifts to become unstoppable.

Ask yourself: Who is one athlete or mentor I can study this week with real focus, and what specific skill do I want to download from them?

Mindset Drill: The 3-Minute Engraving Session

Do this before practice or training so the image is fresh when your body attempts the skill.

» Minute 1: Select and Watch.
Pick ONE specific skill you want to improve. Not your whole game. One skill. Find real game footage or professional training footage of a pro performing that skill. Watch it three times. First time: absorb the full movement. Second time: focus on one body part (feet, hands, hips, or eyes). Third time: trace the complete chain of movement from start to finish.

» Minute 2: Engrave.
Close your eyes. Replay the skill in your mind like a mental video. Can you see it clearly? If it's blurry, open your eyes, watch one more time, then close them again. Repeat until the image is sharp. That sharp mental picture IS the HD blueprint being installed into your brain's motor circuits.

» Minute 3: Merge.
Eyes still closed. Now picture YOURSELF performing that exact skill. In your uniform. On your court or field. In your next game. Don't see the pro anymore. See YOU doing what the pro does. Feel it in your hands, your feet, your whole body. Merge their blueprint with your identity. Then go practice it for real.

❌ Pro Tip: Stack this with your morning Declaration Drill from Chapter 1, or do it separately right before you train. And remember: watch REAL game footage, not influencer content. Full quarters. Full rounds. Real pressure. The cleaner the download, the better your body runs the program. KD watched full games of Dirk. Fury watched hundreds of rounds of Klitschko. Give your brain something excellent to absorb, and it will reward you on the court, the field, or the ring.

Chapter Summary

Kevin Durant couldn't bench 185 at the combine, but he studied Dirk, Kobe, MJ, and Bird frame by frame and became one of the most unstoppable scorers ever. Tyson Fury studied months of Klitschko footage and outboxed a champion nobody could beat. The engraving technique proves your brain builds real skill blueprints through focused observation. Gallwey proved a total beginner improved dramatically from just twenty minutes of intentional watching. Stop scrolling trick shot reels and start studying real pros in real games. Humility is the willingness to learn from someone ahead of you. Every GOAT was a student first.

If You Want to Dive Deeper

Check out The Inner Game of Tennis by Timothy Gallwey, the coach behind the famous 60 Minutes experiment.

3

SEE VICTORY FIRST – TIM TEBOW

"Now faith is confidence in what we hope for and assurance about what we do not see." — *Hebrews 11:1*

You know that feeling in a movie when the hero closes their eyes right before the final battle? Everything goes quiet. The music drops low. And you can almost see the plan forming behind their eyelids like a hologram loading up. Think Doctor Strange scanning 14 million futures. Think Black Panther in the ancestral plane, downloading wisdom before the fight of his life.

That's not just Hollywood magic. That's a real skill. And one of the most doubted, most disrespected, most underestimated athletes in modern sports used it to pull off a play that left an entire nation speechless.

Let's talk about Tim Tebow.

January 8th, 2012. Mile High Stadium, Denver. The NFL Wild Card playoffs. The Denver Broncos versus the Pittsburgh Steelers, one of the most feared defenses on the planet. And standing behind center for Denver is a quarterback that basically every football analyst in America said did not belong there.

Tim Tebow. The guy with the "broken" throwing motion. The guy ESPN ran whole segments about just to explain why he would fail. The guy draft experts called a project, a gimmick, a college system quarterback who would get swallowed alive in the pros.

Skip Bayless was one of the only people on TV defending him, and even that felt lonely.

But here's the thing about Tim Tebow. While the critics were busy making graphics about his bad mechanics, Tebow was doing something they couldn't measure on any scouting report.

He was seeing the win before the whistle.

Overtime. First play. Tebow drops back, feels the pocket, and launches a pass to Demaryius Thomas on a quick slant. Thomas catches it in stride, breaks a tackle, and takes off. Eighty yards. Touchdown. Game over. The stadium literally shakes. Confetti erupts. Tebow drops to one knee on the field, hand on his forehead, eyes closed, thanking God while the whole world watches with their jaws on the floor.

Eighty yards. One play. Against the Pittsburgh Steelers. In overtime. In the playoffs.

And Tebow had already seen the whole thing.

Not in a crystal ball. Not in some weird mystical experience. In his mind. Before every game, Tim Tebow would sit in a quiet place, close his eyes, and visualize the entire game with insane detail. We're talking the feel of the football laces pressing into his fingertips. The sound of the crowd building like a wave. The smell of the turf. The rush of cold Denver air against his face mask. He didn't just picture highlights. He mentally rehearsed full drives, play by play, feeling every emotion along the way.

But here's what separated Tebow from every other athlete doing visualization: he visualized with prayer. He didn't just see himself winning. He saw himself performing while completely surrendered to God. He saw the plays, felt the pressure, and then handed the whole movie reel over to the Creator of the universe and said, "It's Yours."

That's what "Tebowing" was. When he dropped to one knee on the sideline or in the end zone, that wasn't a stunt. That wasn't for cameras. That was the physical expression of a man who had already seen the whole game in his mind, already given it to God, and was now just walking through what he'd already rehearsed in faith.

Was Tim Tebow the most talented quarterback in the NFL? Not even close. Was he the most mentally and spiritually prepared player on the field? Every. Single. Time.

And that made all the difference.

Now let me bring this into your world, because this is where it gets crazy good.

Most people think visualization is just "picturing stuff." Like closing your eyes and vaguely imagining yourself scoring a goal. That's daydreaming. That's screensaver mode. Real visualization, the kind that actually rewires your brain and crushes anxiety, uses all five senses. Every single one.

See the field. The jersey colors. The scoreboard with the time ticking down. See the faces of your teammates, the ref's hand signals, the way the light hits the gym floor.

Hear the crowd noise building. Your coach yelling from the sideline. The squeak of sneakers on hardwood. The thud of the ball. The whistle.

Feel the ball in your hands. The grip of your cleats digging into turf. The sweat on your forehead. The tension in your legs right before you explode off the line.

Smell the freshly cut grass. The rubber of the gym. The chalk dust. The locker room before warm-ups.

And then the secret weapon that locks it all in: emotion. Don't just see yourself making the play. FEEL the confidence surging through your chest. Feel the calm washing over you like you've done this a thousand times. Feel the joy, the fire, the quiet certainty that says, "I was made for this moment."

The emotion is what cements the visualization deep into your subconscious. Without it, you're just watching a mental movie. With it, you're programming your brain to perform.

Here's a bonus technique that elite athletes use, and it's so simple it feels like cheating. Before you visualize yourself performing a skill, give your brain a blueprint first. Find real game footage of a pro performing that exact skill. Not a random TikTok compilation.

Actual game film.

Watch it three to five times. Slow it down. Notice the footwork, the hand placement, the hip rotation, the timing. Your brain has something called mirror neurons. When you watch someone else perform a movement, those neurons fire as if YOU were doing it, creating a mental template in your mind. Scientists discovered this back in 1996 and it changed everything we know about learning.

Once you've studied the pro footage, THEN close your eyes and visualize yourself performing that same skill. Your jersey. Your court. Your game. You just gave your brain a high-definition target to aim for instead of a blurry guess.

But here's the part most people skip, and it might be the most important piece of the whole puzzle.

Visualize failure too.

Not to be negative. To be prepared. See yourself throwing an interception, then immediately making a game-saving tackle on the runback. See yourself missing the first free throw, then calmly draining the second one with pure confidence. See yourself striking out, then ripping a double your next time at bat.

Because here's reality: the game WILL throw curveballs at you. If you've only ever visualized perfection, your brain panics the second something goes wrong. It has no file saved for that situation. But if you've already rehearsed the comeback? Your brain has a plan. It stays calm. It executes.

Proverbs 24:16 says it perfectly: "For though the righteous fall seven times, they rise again." The righteous don't avoid falling. They've already rehearsed what rising looks like. That falling and rising? That's part of the vision too.

And look at Hebrews 11:1 one more time. "Faith is confidence in what we hope for and assurance about what we do not see." Read that slowly. Faith is seeing the unseen as already real. Tebow saw the touchdown before the snap. He felt the victory before the whistle. That's not arrogance. That's not wishful thinking. That's Hebrews 11:1 in a helmet and shoulder pads.

So when you're lying in bed the night before a big game and the anxiety starts creeping in like that weird feeling before a boss fight, remember this: your brain cannot tell the difference between a vivid mental rehearsal and the real thing. If you've already "been there" fifty times in your mind, the big moment doesn't feel unfamiliar anymore. And unfamiliar is what triggers fear. Familiar is what triggers confidence. You're not removing the pressure. You're making the pressure feel like home.

Tebow wasn't the fastest, the strongest, or the most mechanically gifted. But he stepped into every game having already lived it in his mind and surrendered it in prayer. That combination is absolutely unstoppable. And you have access to the exact same tools right now.

The Science Behind Visualization

Here's why this works on a brain level, and it's honestly wild. When you vividly visualize a movement, your brain fires the exact same motor neurons as when you physically perform it. Scientists proved this back in 1994, and it's been confirmed over and over since then. Your nervous system literally cannot tell the difference between a detailed mental rehearsal and the real deal.

A study from the Cleveland Clinic took it even further. People who only mentally practiced a muscle contraction, never actually moving, increased their strength by 13.5 percent. Just from thinking about it. With vivid detail. Consistently.

Now think about what this means for performance anxiety. Your brain has a fear center called the amygdala. Its whole job is to flag unfamiliar situations as threats. Big game? Huge crowd? Sudden pressure? If your brain hasn't "experienced" that before, the amygdala sounds the alarm and floods your body with stress hormones. But if you've visualized that exact moment fifty times with all five senses and real emotion, your amygdala stays quiet. It recognizes the situation. It's been here before. Familiar isn't scary. Familiar is fuel.

Prayer

Lord, give me the faith to see what You've planned before it unfolds. Calm my anxiety and help me trust the vision You've placed inside me. Amen.

Tim Tebow was told by every expert that he couldn't succeed. He responded by visualizing victory with prayer, surrendering the outcome to God, and showing up more mentally prepared than anyone on the field.

Ask yourself: What upcoming moment am I anxious about, and what if I spent three minutes tonight seeing myself walking through it with calm, confidence, and faith?

Mindset Drill: The 3-Minute Mental Game Film

This is your pre-game cheat code. Do it the night before competition or during quiet time before warm-ups.

» Minute 1: Build the Scene. Close your eyes. Construct your next game environment with all five senses. See the court or field, the lights, the colors. Hear the crowd and the whistle. Feel the ball, the ground under your feet, the temperature. Smell the gym or the grass. Drop yourself fully into that moment. Pro tip: if there's a specific skill you want to nail, watch real game footage of a pro doing it once before you close your eyes. Let your mirror neurons build the blueprint.

» Minute 2: See the Skill. Visualize yourself performing ONE key skill in perfect form. Run it in slow motion first, noticing every detail. Then run it at full speed. Most importantly, feel the emotion. Feel the confidence radiating through your body. Feel the calm. Feel the joy of executing exactly how you trained. Let that emotion lock the image deep into your memory.

» Minute 3: See the Comeback. Now visualize ONE thing going wrong. A missed shot. A bad call. A turnover. See it happen. Then see yourself take one deep breath, reset your posture, and absolutely crush the next play. Always end your mental game film with success. Always. Your brain remembers the last scene the most vividly, so make sure the final frame is you winning.

Pro Tip: Keep it consistent. The more you replay the same visualization, the deeper it's engraved in your brain. Tebow didn't visualize once before a game. He did it repeatedly, layered with prayer, until the moment felt as familiar as brushing his teeth. Repetition turns visualization from a nice idea into an actual competitive weapon.

Chapter Summary

Visualization is not daydreaming. It's active mental rehearsal using all five senses and real emotion. Your brain fires the same neurons whether you physically perform a skill or vividly imagine it, which means mental reps are real reps. Tim Tebow used this exact approach, combined with prayer and surrender to God, to pull off one of the most shocking plays in NFL playoff history. Use the engraving technique by studying pro footage first. Always visualize recovery from mistakes, not just perfection. And remember Hebrews 11:1: faith is seeing the unseen as already real.

If You Want to Dive Deeper

Grab Mind Gym by Gary Mack for elite-level sports visualization techniques that coaches at every level swear by.

4

WRITE THE VISION – SERENA WILLIAMS

> *"Write down the revelation and make it plain on tablets so that a herald may run with it. For the revelation awaits an appointed time... Though it linger, wait for it; it will certainly come." — Habakkuk 2:2–3*

Imagine a notebook.

Not a fancy leather journal. Not some app with premium features. Just a regular notebook, the kind you grab from the dollar store. Now imagine that inside this notebook is a 78-page handwritten plan for creating two of the greatest athletes planet Earth has ever seen. A plan written before the athletes in question could even crawl.

Sound like science fiction? Nope. That's a true story. And the man who wrote it was sitting in a small house in Compton, California, watching a tennis match on TV.

His name was Richard Williams. And he was about to change sports history with a pen.

Here's the scene. Richard is watching the French Open and sees the winner collect a check for $40,000. At that moment, something clicks. He turns to his wife, Oracene, and basically says, "Our daughters are going to be tennis champions." The wild part? Venus and Serena weren't even born yet. He hadn't picked up a tennis racket in his life. He was living in one of the roughest neighborhoods in America. Zero tennis connections. Zero coaching experience. Zero reasons for anyone to believe him.

But Richard didn't just dream it. He grabbed a notebook and wrote a 78-page plan. Every detail. The training schedule. The tournaments. The goals. The step-by-step vision for how two little girls from Compton would dominate a sport that had never seen anyone who looked like them at the top.

Then he posted those goals in big, bold letters on the walls of their home.

Every. Single. Day. Venus and Serena woke up and saw their future staring back at them, written in their father's handwriting. Not "maybe one day." Not "wouldn't it be cool if." The words on those walls read like it was already done. Like the universe just hadn't caught up yet.

Fast forward to Serena Williams standing on Centre Court at Wimbledon, holding trophy number 23. Twenty-three Grand Slam singles titles. The greatest female tennis player of all time. And honestly? One of the greatest athletes, period. Full stop.

But here's the part that turns this from an incredible sports story into something deeper. Something that hits your soul.

Serena didn't just coast on talent. Life came for her. Hard. She battled injuries that would've retired most players. She lost matches that broke her heart on the world's biggest stages. She nearly died during childbirth because of a pulmonary embolism, which is basically a blood clot that threatens your life. She had an emergency C-section, fought through recovery, and then came BACK to professional tennis. At 35. And won.

Through all of it, Serena held onto her faith like a lifeline. She's talked openly about how God carried her when her body couldn't carry itself. She once said, "I've always believed I could do anything because I was raised to believe it, and I saw it written down."

Read that again slowly. She saw it written down.

Not just thought about it. Not just wished for it in the shower. She SAW it. On the walls. In the notebooks. In the plan her father created before she existed. Her goals were written, spoken, and backed by faith. That combination? Almost unfair.

Now look at Habakkuk 2:2. God literally told the prophet, "Write the vision down. Make it plain." Not "think good thoughts." Not "manifest positive vibes." Write. It. Down. And then the part every young athlete needs to tattoo on their brain: "Though it linger, wait for it; it will certainly come."

That means your goals might not happen on your timeline. Serena didn't win her first Grand Slam until she was 17, and her journey from Compton's cracked public courts to Centre Court took years of grinding that nobody saw. The wait is not the problem. Quitting during the wait is the problem.

So let's bring this right to your locker, your bedroom, your life.

You've got dreams. I know you do. Maybe it's making varsity. Maybe it's earning a scholarship. Maybe it's just proving to yourself that you're not the person that last bad game said you were. But here's the honest truth that most people won't tell you: a dream without ink is just a wish. And wishes don't have game plans.

Richard Williams didn't wish his daughters into greatness. He wrote a 78-page blueprint. Serena didn't hope her faith would be enough. She combined belief with written, visible, daily goals. And God Himself, when He wanted to communicate the most important vision in history, told the prophet to grab a pen.

There is something almost supernatural about writing your goals down. And it's not just spiritual. Science backs it up too.

Here's the real talk though. Most goal-setting advice tells you to "just stay positive!" Visualize success! Think happy thoughts! And look, positivity matters. But if that's ALL you do, you're building a house with no foundation. Because obstacles are coming. They always do. Serena didn't avoid obstacles. She planned for them. And that's the upgrade most people miss.

So your goals need two things: a clear target AND a plan for when life tries to knock you off course. Write the dream. Then write the dragon standing between you and the dream. Then write exactly how you're going to slay it before it shows up.

That's not negativity. That's wisdom with a strategy.

God built celebrations into the Israelite calendar after every harvest, every victory, every deliverance. He knows humans need to mark progress. When you hit a milestone, celebrate it. A favorite meal. A movie night. New gear. A full rest day with zero guilt. Nehemiah 8:10 says, "The joy of the Lord is your strength." Joy isn't a luxury for after you've made it. Joy is rocket fuel for the journey.

Richard Williams celebrated small wins with Venus and Serena constantly. Every improvement. Every milestone. Because he understood that the path to 23 Grand Slams starts with celebrating the first clean backhand on a cracked Compton court.

Your written vision is your blueprint. Your faith is the foundation. Your daily action is the brick. And your celebration is the proof that it's working.

The Science Behind Writing It Down

Here's why a pen is more powerful than a thought. Writing activates both hemispheres of your brain. The left side handles logic and language. The right side handles creativity and emotion. When you just think about a goal, you only light up one side. When you write it, your entire brain locks in.

Scientists call this the "generation effect" (Slamecka & Graf, 1978). Information you produce by writing sticks in your memory significantly better than information you passively hear or read. Writing also fires up your reticular activating system, your brain's search engine, programming it to filter your world for opportunities that match your goals.

And timing matters. Morning and night, your brain operates in a theta wave state, which is basically your most programmable mode. That's why checking your phone first thing in the morning is so dangerous. You're handing VIP backstage access to your subconscious over to whatever the algorithm decides to show you. Instead, write your vision first. Let YOUR goals be the first thing your mind processes.

Psychologist Gabriele Oettingen at NYU developed a method called WOOP: Wish, Outcome, Obstacle, Plan. Her research found that writing your goal PLUS the biggest obstacle PLUS an "if/then" plan outperforms pure positive visualization by a significant margin. Your brain gets prepared for resistance instead of blindsided by it.

Prayer

Lord, give me the honesty to name my dreams and the perseverance to chase them daily. Let my written vision honor You. Amen.

Reflection: The Serena Williams Lesson

Richard Williams wrote his daughters' future on paper and walls before they could walk. Serena absorbed that written vision, combined it with unshakable faith, and became the greatest. Written goals backed by belief create an almost unstoppable force.

Ask yourself: What's one goal I've been carrying only in my head that needs to hit paper today?

Mindset Drill: The 3-Minute Vision Journal Sprint

This is your daily blueprint session. Grab a notebook. Same one, every day. Make it yours.

» Minute 1: Write ONE major goal for this season.
Follow the 6 Rules of Unshakable Goal Writing:

» Present tense. "I am a varsity starter averaging 12 points per game by February." Not "I will make varsity."

» Positive action. "I sink free throws with confidence." Not "I won't miss free throws." Your brain can't process negatives. (Don't think about a pink elephant. What did you just picture? Exactly.)

» Specific. "I run the 40 in 4.8 seconds by March 1st." Not "I want to be faster."

» Measurable. Attach numbers, dates, or visible outcomes.

» Make your BIG goal unreasonable. If it doesn't scare you a little, it's too small. David's goal of fighting Goliath was insane. It was also God-sized.

» Make your DAILY goal bite-sized. Small. Controllable. Completable. "Today I take 50 extra shots after practice."

Minute 2: Write the ONE biggest obstacle that could stop you. Then write your if/then plan: "If I feel too tired and want to skip extra reps, THEN I will remember Serena came back from an emergency C-section and won at 35." This is the Obstacle Upgrade. It doesn't make you negative. It makes you ready.

Then write ONE thing you'll do TODAY to move toward the goal. Just one. Bite-sized. Something you can finish before your head hits the pillow.

Minute 3: Write one Scripture underneath everything. If you're stuck, start with Habakkuk 2:2 or Philippians 4:13. Then read everything you just wrote. Out loud if you can. Let your own handwriting preach back to you.

Pro Tip: Do this in the morning BEFORE your phone. Your brain is in theta state, wide open, and programmable. Don't let TikTok write your code for the day. YOU write it. And at night before sleep, read it again. Bookend your day with YOUR vision, not the world's noise.

❎ Celebrate Wins: When you hit a milestone, mark it. Circle it in your journal. Treat yourself. Richard Williams celebrated every small victory with Venus and Serena because he knew joy builds momentum. Don't wait until the Grand Slam. Celebrate the first clean serve.

Chapter Summary

Serena Williams grew up seeing her future written on the walls of her home because her father, Richard, created a 78-page handwritten plan before she was even born. That written vision, combined with deep faith and relentless daily action, produced 23 Grand Slam titles. Writing goals activates your whole brain. Thinking alone only uses half. Write in present tense, positive action, specific, and measurable. Add the obstacle plus your if/then plan because research shows it outperforms pure positive thinking. And celebrate every milestone along the way. Joy is fuel, not a luxury.

If you want to level up, you need to stop just "vibing" and start mapping. Dive into The Mamba Mentality to see how Kobe Bryant used a notebook like a cheat code, literally sketching out his opponents' weaknesses and scripting his own moves before he ever stepped on the court. Or, if you want a step-by-step guide to hacking your own brain, check out The Champion's Mind by Jim Afremow.

5

BREATHE UNDER PRESSURE – MANNY PACQUIAO

> *"For God has not given us a spirit of fear, but of power and of love and of a sound mind." — 2 Timothy 1:7*

Your breath is a superpower nobody told you about.

Not laser eyes. Not super speed. Something way more useful. Something you carry into every game, every test, every moment your heart starts pounding and your brain screams "YOU'RE CHOKING." Something so powerful that Navy SEALs use it under actual gunfire, and one of the most dangerous boxers who ever lived used it between rounds against men who wanted to rearrange his face.

Let's talk about Manny Pacquiao. Again. Because this man's story just keeps delivering.

Picture this: MGM Grand Garden Arena, Las Vegas. Fifteen thousand screaming fans packed shoulder to shoulder. Camera flashes popping like lightning. The air smells like sweat and adrenaline and money. Across the ring stands Oscar De La Hoya, one of the most decorated boxers in history. Bigger. Heavier. A betting favorite. And Manny? Manny is the undersized Filipino fighter that half the boxing world thinks is about to get demolished.

The bell rings. Rounds fly by. Fists crack against jaw bones. Manny is taking shots, landing shots, moving like a video game character who found the speed boost. But here's the part the cameras almost missed, the part that changed everything.

Between rounds, while De La Hoya sat on his stool gasping, eyes wide, chest heaving like he just sprinted uphill, Manny did something completely different. He sat down. Closed his eyes. Breathed slowly. And prayed.

That's it. Breathe. Pray. Reset.

No panic. No rushing. Just a skinny kid from General Santos City in the Philippines connecting with the God who gave him every breath he'd ever taken. And then? He opened his eyes, stood up, and went back out there with peace on his face like he was walking into church, not a boxing ring.

De La Hoya's corner stopped the fight after round eight. Manny won. And the boxing world lost its mind.

But rewind even further. Before the bright lights and the belt buckles and the millions, Manny Pacquiao was a fourteen year old kid who hadn't eaten in two days. He left his family's home with nothing. No coach. No gym. No money. He moved to Manila and survived on the streets, fighting not for glory but for his next meal. The kind of stress most of us will never know.

And somewhere in that darkness, Manny learned something that would carry him through eight world championships in eight different weight divisions (something literally no other boxer in history has done). He learned that when everything around you is chaos, the one thing you can always control is your next breath.

He's said it plain: "Before every round, I give it to God. I breathe, I pray, and I go back out there with peace."

Manny is now a born-again Christian and an ordained pastor. He reads his Bible daily. He's fought the most dangerous human beings on the planet. And his secret weapon was never his legendary left hand. It was his breath and his faith working together like a one-two combo straight to fear's chin.

Now let me bring in someone from a totally different arena. Kevin

Durant. KD. One of the most gifted scorers basketball has ever seen and also one of the most attacked athletes on the internet. When he left Oklahoma City for Golden State, half the sports world called him a snake. Burner account scandals. Memes. Social media attacks daily. The kind of hate that would make most people crawl under a blanket and never come out.

But watch KD in a close playoff game. Game 3 of the 2017 NBA Finals. Clock winding down. The Warriors need a bucket. And KD pulls up for a three pointer over LeBron James. LEBRON. The most intimidating defender on earth is right in his face. And KD's body looks like he's shooting in an empty gym. Still. Calm. Composed. Nothing but net. Championship sealed.

That stillness doesn't come from nowhere. KD has Proverbs 15:33 tattooed on his body: "Before honor comes humility." That verse lives in his skin. And that composure you see in crunch time? That's a man who learned to control what's happening inside when everything outside is screaming.

Okay. Time out. Let's bring this to YOUR life.

Every other chapter in this book gives you tools for before the game. Morning declarations. Visualization. Goals. Those are your pre-game power ups. But what happens when you're IN the game and everything goes sideways? You miss three shots in a row. The crowd gets loud and hostile. Your coach is yelling. That voice in your head starts whispering, "You're blowing it."

THAT is the moment most athletes fall apart. Not because they lack talent. Because they have no tool for pressure that hits in real time. They trained their body but never trained their breath.

Here's what's wild. Breathing is the ONLY function in your body that is both automatic AND controllable. Your heart beats on its own and you can't just tell it to slow down. Your stomach digests on its own. But your breath? You breathe without thinking every single day, AND you can choose to breathe differently whenever you want. That means your breath is a bridge. A literal bridge between your panicking body and your thinking brain.

When you take control of your breath, you take control of your nervous system. When you control your nervous system, you control your performance. Period.

Think about Genesis 2:7: "Then the Lord God formed a man from the dust of the ground and breathed into his nostrils the breath of life, and the man became a living being." The very first thing God ever gave you wasn't a thought. Wasn't a feeling. It was a breath. The Hebrew word for Spirit is "ruach," and it literally means breath or wind. Your breath isn't just biology. It's the original gift from your Creator.

And in John 20:22, Jesus breathed on His disciples and said, "Receive the Holy Spirit." Power came through breath. Peace came through breath. Your reset in the fourth quarter comes through breath too.

So next time you're standing at the free throw line with the game on the line, or stepping up to the plate with two outs, or walking into a room where everyone expects you to fail, remember this: the same God who breathed life into the first human being gave you the ability to reset yourself in a single breath. Manny used it against the most dangerous fighters alive. KD used it over LeBron in the Finals. You can use it in your next game, your next test, your next hard conversation.

Breathe. Pray. Reset. Go.

The Science Behind the Breath (Why This Actually Works)

When stress hits, your sympathetic nervous system fires up. That's your fight or flight mode. Heart rate spikes. Muscles tighten. Vision narrows. Fine motor skills drop. That's why your shot feels totally different in a packed gym versus an empty one. Same arm, same ball, different nervous system.

Box breathing (4 seconds in, 4 seconds hold, 4 seconds out, 4 seconds hold) activates your parasympathetic nervous system, your body's built in "calm down" system, within 60 seconds (Ma et al., 2017). Navy SEALs use this under live gunfire. If it calms a soldier getting shot at, it will calm you at the free throw line.

The physiological sigh, a double inhale through your nose followed by one long exhale through your mouth, is the fastest known way to reduce stress in real time. Stanford neuroscientist Andrew Huberman's lab proved it works in a single breath cycle. One breath. That's your between plays reset.

And Wim Hof, the "Iceman," built an entire performance method around controlled breathing, proving through university research that breath patterns can directly influence stress hormones and even the immune system. You don't need ice baths. But the science confirms what Manny already knew: your breath is a remote control for your entire body. Learn to use it.

Prayer

Lord, when pressure hits, remind me that my next breath is Your gift. Fill me with Your peace and power to stay calm and courageous. Amen.

Reflection: The Manny Pacquiao and Kevin Durant Lesson

Manny breathes and prays between rounds against the most dangerous fighters alive. KD stays still and composed over LeBron with a championship on the line. Both chose calm when chaos was screaming.

Ask yourself: When pressure hit me last, did I react on panic or respond with a breath? What if one breath could change everything?

Mindset Drill: The 3-Minute Reset Breath (Two Modes)

This is your real time weapon. The tool that works DURING the fight, not just before it.

Pre-Game Version (3 Minutes):

Sit or stand with your eyes closed. Feet flat. Hands relaxed.

Do 4 cycles of box breathing: breathe in for 4 counts, hold for 4, breathe out for 4, hold for 4. That's one cycle.

Between each cycle, say one short phrase out loud or in your mind: "God has not given me a spirit of fear."

After 4 full cycles, open your eyes. You're reset. You're ready. Walk out there different.

In-Game Version (10 Seconds):

Between plays. Before a free throw. Between pitches. Between points. Waiting for the next serve.

Do ONE physiological sigh: double inhale through your nose (quick sniff-sniff), then one long slow exhale through your mouth. One single rep. Six to ten seconds total. Done.

You just told your nervous system: "We're good. Next play."

Pro Tip: Practice BOTH versions every single day so they become automatic. Don't wait for game pressure to try this for the first time. Manny didn't learn to breathe and pray during a title fight. He practiced it so many times that when the bell rang, his body already knew what to do. Make your calm a habit, not a wish.

Chapter Summary

Breathing is the ONLY body function that is both automatic and controllable, making it your bridge between panic and peak performance. Manny Pacquiao used breath and prayer between rounds against the most dangerous fighters on earth. Kevin Durant stayed composed over LeBron with a title on the line. Box breathing resets your nervous system in 60 seconds. The physiological sigh resets you in one single breath. And God's very first gift to humanity was breath itself (Genesis 2:7). Your calm is closer than you think. It's one breath away.

If You Want to Dive Deeper:

Read Breath by James Nestor. It's the best book on how breathing shapes performance and health. Also check out The Wim Hof Method by Wim Hof and Andrew Huberman's free YouTube episodes on the physiological sigh. Game changers, all of them.

6

QUIET MIND SPEED – USAIN BOLT

You know what's absolutely wild? The fastest human being who ever lived won races by being the most relaxed person on the track.

Not the most tense. Not the most amped up. The most calm.

Picture this: Beijing. London. Rio. Three different Olympic Games. The 100-meter final. The biggest, loudest, most pressure-packed 10 seconds in all of sports. Eighty thousand people screaming so loud the stadium literally vibrates under your feet. A billion viewers watching on screens around the planet. Eight men in the final, every single one of them the fastest human in their entire country. Muscles coiled like loaded springs. Jaws clenched. Eyes locked with laser focus. Hearts pounding through their chests.

And then there's this six-foot-five Jamaican kid in Lane 5. Dancing. Literally dancing. Waving at the camera. Blowing kisses to the crowd. Grinning like he's at a house party and his favorite song just came on.

His name? Usain Bolt. Sprinter. Legend. The Lightning Bolt himself.

And while the world thought he was just showing off, what he was actually doing was something way more powerful. He was entering the zone.

Let's rewind the tape. Usain Bolt grew up in Sherwood Content, a tiny rural town tucked into the hills of Trelawny, Jamaica. We're talking small. Like, "everybody knows everybody's grandma" small. He grew up in church. His parents, Wellesley and Jennifer Bolt, raised him in faith. Before every race, if you watched closely, you'd see Usain cross himself and look up. Quick. Quiet. Real. He wasn't performing for the cameras. He was talking to God.

But here's where the story gets real. People forget that Bolt's road to dominance was full of potholes. As a teenager, he dealt with scoliosis, a curvature of his spine that caused serious back pain and made his running mechanics uneven. Coaches constantly worried his body would break down. In 2004, at just 18 years old, he went to the Athens Olympics loaded with hype as Jamaica's next big thing. He got hurt. Got eliminated early. Went home embarrassed. The whole island had been watching, and he flopped.

Imagine that pressure. Your entire country pins their hopes on you, and you crash.

Most people would've come back tighter. More stressed. More desperate to prove themselves. That's what pressure does to most athletes. It makes them grip harder, clench their fists, tighten every muscle, and try to force results. And that's exactly what kills performance.

But Bolt learned something that most sprinters never figure out: tension is the enemy of speed. Every muscle you clench that doesn't need to be clenched is a brake pedal. Your body can't fire at full power when your mind is full of noise. A worried brain sends stress signals that literally tighten your muscles and slow your reaction time. It's like trying to sprint through mud.

So Bolt did the opposite of what anxiety tells you to do. He got quiet inside.

Before every Olympic final, after all the dancing and waving, there was a moment. The stadium would hush. The starter would call "Set." And Bolt would drop into the blocks, close his eyes for just a beat, and go completely still. Everything left. The crowd, the cameras, the seven other fastest men on earth crouching beside him. Gone. In that instant, only the race existed. Only the feel of his spikes pressed against the blocks. Only the lane ahead.

Then the gun fired. And the world watched a man run 9.58

seconds in the 100 meters, a record that still stands and might stand forever.

That wasn't talent alone. That was a quiet mind unleashing what a loud mind would have caged.

Now let's bring this right to your life. Because I know this feeling, and I bet you do too.

You're standing at the free throw line with two seconds left and your team down by one. Or you're in the batter's box with runners on base. Or you're about to serve for the match. And suddenly your brain goes full group chat. Every notification at once. "Don't miss." "Everyone's watching." "What if I choke?" "Coach is gonna bench me." "My parents are in the stands."

That noise? That's not focus. That's mental clutter. And it does to your performance exactly what scoliosis did to Bolt's spine. It throws everything off.

Here's the truth that changed everything for me and will change everything for you: you don't need to be louder to perform better. You need to be quieter. Isaiah 30:15 says it plain: "In quietness and trust is your strength." God didn't design your best performance to come from panic. He designed it to come from peace.

Think about that for a second. Quietness IS strength. Not weakness. Not laziness. Strength. The strongest athletes on earth, the ones who perform their best when everything is on the line, are the ones who've trained their minds to get still.

And here's the part that connects to your actual skill work, because this isn't just about calming down. It's about how you practice.

You ever been in a slump? That stretch where everything feels off and nothing works no matter how hard you try? Your shot won't fall. Your swing feels weird. Your passes are off. And the harder you push, the worse it gets? That's not you losing your talent. That's a corrupted file in your brain.

Let me explain. When you practice a movement, your brain wraps a substance called myelin around that neural pathway. Myelin is like insulation on a wire. The thicker the myelin, the faster and smoother the signal travels, and the more automatic the skill becomes. That's literally what "muscle memory" is.

But here's the catch: myelin doesn't know the difference between a good rep and a bad rep. If you practice fast and sloppy, your brain wraps myelin around the sloppy version. Now the wrong movement feels natural. That's a slump. Your brain locked in a glitch.

The fix? Go slow. Like, painfully slow. Strip the skill down to its most basic form. Perform it at 25% speed. Feel every muscle. Notice your balance, your hands, your breathing. Let your brain find the glitch and rebuild the correct pathway, rep by rep. It feels like going backward. It requires serious humility. But when your phone freezes, you don't chuck it in the trash. You restart it. Slow practice is a reboot for your skills.

Colossians 3:23 says, "Whatever you do, work at it with all your heart, as working for the Lord." And "all your heart" doesn't mean "as fast as possible." It means with full attention. Full care. Full intention. Three slow, perfect reps are worth more than thirty fast, messy ones.

So here's the elite combo that separates good athletes from legendary ones: meditate first, then practice slow. Clear the mind, then build the skill. When your brain is still and your reps are deliberate, the myelin wraps thicker and cleaner. The pathway gets built right. And when you finally add speed? It flows. Effortlessly. Like Bolt gliding down that track with the biggest grin on the planet.

Speed is the last ingredient. Not the first. Accuracy builds the road. Speed just drives on it.

And the coolest part? Galatians 6:9 promises: "Let us not become weary in doing good, for at the proper time we will reap a harvest if we do not give up." Slow practice doesn't feel glamorous. Nobody's posting their slow motion reps on TikTok. But the harvest is coming. The breakthrough is loading. Keep going.

Bolt looked relaxed in those Olympic finals because his mind was quiet. Not because the moment was small. The moment was enormous. But his inner world was still. He had already done the work, already prayed, already surrendered the outcome to God. So when the gun fired, there was nothing left to fight. Just run.

You can have that same stillness. Not one day when you're famous. Right now. Today. In your next practice. In your next game. In the next moment when the pressure squeezes and your brain starts screaming.

Be still. And watch what God does through a quiet mind.

The Science Behind the Stillness

Research by Scott-Hamilton (2017) found that athletes who practiced mindfulness meditation entered flow states significantly more often and performed at higher levels under pressure. Flow, what athletes call "the zone," is total absorption, loss of self-consciousness, and effortless focus (Csikszentmihalyi, 1990). It's the state where time slows down and everything clicks. Meditation is the most reliable gateway to getting there consistently.

On the practice side, Daniel Coyle's research in The Talent Code (2009) showed that deliberate, accurate repetitions increase myelin density far more efficiently than fast, sloppy ones. Quality of reps beats quantity every single time. Your brain literally builds stronger wiring around movements performed slowly and correctly. That's why master musicians practice scales in slow motion and elite shooters rebuild their form frame by frame. Slow is smooth, and smooth eventually becomes fast. Combine a clear mind with deliberate practice and you've got the formula that built champions from Michael Jordan to Usain Bolt.

Prayer

Lord, quiet my mind so my body can do what You built it to do. Help me trust the stillness. In Jesus' name, Amen.

Reflection: The Usain Bolt Lesson

Bolt didn't win eight Olympic golds by being the most stressed sprinter on the track. He won by being the most still inside. His quiet mind freed his body to fly.

Ask yourself: Where in my game am I gripping too tight, and what would happen if I let my mind get quiet instead?

This is your pre-practice power-down. Think of it like putting your brain in airplane mode so it can actually lock in.

Step 1: Find your spot. Somewhere quiet. Your room, the locker room before anyone else shows up, even your car before practice. Sit or stand. Set a timer for 3 minutes.

Step 2: Close your eyes and picture a calm river. Clear water, smooth rocks, gentle current. This is your mind.

Step 3: Every thought that floats in, attach it to a log and let it drift downstream. "I bombed that test." Log. Gone. "What if coach yells at me?" Log. Gone. The goal isn't an empty river. It's fewer logs than yesterday.

Step 4: When the timer goes off, take one deep breath in through your nose, out through your mouth, open your eyes, and go practice ONE skill.

Step 5: Slow it down. Perform your skill at 25% speed for 3 to 5 reps. Feel everything. Then build to 50%. Then 75%. Only go full speed if 75% felt clean and smooth. If it didn't? Stay slow. Come back tomorrow. No rushing. No ego. Just mastery.

Pro Tip: If you're in a slump, this drill is your best friend. Don't fight the slump with more intensity. Restart the system with stillness and slow reps. Bolt didn't become the fastest by trying harder. He became the fastest by releasing everything that was slowing him down.

Chapter Summary

Usain Bolt won eight Olympic gold medals not by being the most tense sprinter on the track, but the most calm. His secret was a quiet mind that freed his body to perform at its peak. For young athletes, this means learning to meditate before practice and slowing down skill work to build clean neural pathways. Slumps aren't lost talent; they're corrupted files fixed by slow, deliberate reps. Speed comes last, not first. As Psalm 46:10 reminds us, stillness isn't weakness. It's where God meets your preparation and turns it into something unstoppable.

Check out The Mindful Athlete by George Mumford, the meditation coach behind Michael Jordan, Kobe Bryant, and Shaq. If you want to go VERY deep, read a few pages at a time of "Meditations" by Marcus Aurelius, The great Roman emperor.

7

STRENGTH IN LIMITS – GIANNIS ANTETOKOUNMPO

Picture this. July 20, 2021. Fiserv Forum in Milwaukee. Seventeen thousand fans screaming so loud the floor is vibrating. Game 6 of the NBA Finals. Giannis Antetokounmpo, all six feet eleven inches of pure force, catches the ball near the free throw line, takes two massive strides, rises through three Phoenix Suns defenders like gravity forgot about him, and throws down a block that shakes the entire arena. The building erupts. His teammates are losing their minds. The cameras catch his face and there it is. Not arrogance. Not revenge. Just a kid from Athens who cannot believe this is real.

When the final buzzer sounds, Giannis drops 50 points. Fifty. In a close-out Finals game. He grabs the trophy, holds it like it's made of glass, and says the words that stopped the entire sports world: "I want to thank God for blessing me with this talent."

Then he sobbed. On national television. No shame. Just pure, raw gratitude from a man who knows exactly where he came from.

And where he came from? That's the part that will wreck you.

Rewind to Athens, Greece. Early 2000s. A skinny Nigerian kid named Giannis is walking the streets with his older brother Thanasis, selling watches, sunglasses, and handbags to tourists. Not for fun. For food. His parents, Charles and Veronica, immigrated from Nigeria with almost nothing. They weren't documented. They had no safety net. Some nights, dinner was whatever was cheapest at the market. Some nights, dinner didn't happen.

And here's the detail that lives rent-free in my brain. Giannis and Thanasis shared one pair of basketball shoes. One pair. Between two brothers. They'd literally swap shoes depending on who had practice that day. Imagine showing up to your gym with shoes still warm from your brother's feet because your family can't afford a second pair. That's not a movie scene. That was Tuesday for the Antetokounmpo brothers.

Giannis learned basketball on cracked outdoor courts in Athens with bad lighting and even worse equipment. No personal trainers. No nutritionists. No AAU travel teams or fancy shoe deals. He played in run-down gyms where the rims were slightly bent and the floors were uneven. Everything about his environment screamed "you will never make it."

But here's where it gets superhero-level wild.

Those limitations? They didn't break him. They built him. Every crooked rim taught his brain to adjust. Every tight, crowded court forced him to move faster, think quicker, and play with a kind of creative aggression that you simply cannot learn in a perfect facility. When Giannis arrived in the NBA at eighteen years old, he was raw. His jumper was shaky. His English was rough. But he was fearless, adaptable, and absolutely relentless. Because nothing in a professional basketball arena could be harder than what he had already survived.

Nothing.

After winning that 2021 championship, a reporter asked Giannis if he considered the years before his title to be "failures." His answer became one of the most legendary interview clips ever recorded. He leaned into the mic and said: "It's not a failure. It's steps to success... Michael Jordan played 15 years, won 6 championships. Were the other 9 years failures?"

Silence. The whole room felt that.

Now let me crack this open and show you why it matters for YOUR life.

You know what most athletes think when they don't have the best gear, the best coach, the best facility? They think they're at a disadvantage. They look at the kid with the private lessons and the brand new cleats and think, "Must be nice." And something inside them whispers, "I can't compete with that."

Wrong. Dead wrong. And God's Word proves it.

Open your Bible to Judges chapter 7. God told a warrior named Gideon to go fight a massive enemy army. Gideon had 32,000 soldiers. Pretty solid, right? God said, "Too many. Cut them down." Gideon trimmed it to 10,000. God said, "Still too many." Final number? Three hundred men. Against thousands. And their weapons? Trumpets and clay jars. Not swords. Not shields. Trumpets and jars.

They won.

God has ALWAYS done His greatest work through limitation. A shepherd boy versus a giant. Five loaves feeding five thousand. A kid from Athens sharing shoes with his brother becoming the NBA Finals MVP. When you're working with less, you're actually standing in the exact spot where God loves to show up and show off.

Second Corinthians 12:9 is not just a nice verse for a poster. It's an operational blueprint. "My power is made perfect in weakness." That means your lack is not your ceiling. It's your launching pad. When you have less, you lean harder on God. When you lean harder on God, you access power that kids with every advantage in the world never tap into.

So let's get tactical. Because this isn't just motivation. This is a training weapon.

Pillar one: play small on purpose. When you shrink your tools and your space, your brain has to work overtime and it gets razor sharp. Dribble with a tennis ball and suddenly a basketball feels glued to your hand. Hit bottle caps with a broomstick and a baseball looks like a watermelon. Train with a smaller, heavier ball and the regulation one feels like a feather. Pelé, Messi, Neymar, Ronaldinho all grew up playing Futsal on tiny courts. In Futsal you touch the ball 600% more than regular soccer and make decisions twice as fast. When they stepped onto full-size pitches, the game felt like slow motion. Giannis learned basketball on tight, crowded Athens courts. When he got to the wide-open NBA floor, everything felt spacious.

And here's the teamwork piece. Playing small, like 3v3 instead of 5v5, forces real connection. You cannot hide. Everyone has to contribute. Everyone has to communicate. Trust is not optional. It's survival. Ecclesiastes 4:9-10 says it straight: "Two are better than one... If either of them falls down, one can help the other up."

Pillar two: train rough on purpose. Muhammad Ali trained in the woods of Deer Lake, Pennsylvania. Old equipment. Rocky roads. No luxury. He chose discomfort because he knew something most people miss. When you train in cushy environments, your brain enters maintenance mode. It thinks you're safe, so it coasts. When you train in uncomfortable environments, your brain flips into survival mode. Sharper instincts. Faster adaptation. More creative problem-solving. Manny Pacquiao trained in a dirt-floor gym in General Santos City with almost no equipment. He once said: "I didn't become great despite having nothing. I became great BECAUSE of having nothing."

Train on uneven ground. Practice in wind. Do your skill work at the end of a workout when you're exhausted, not when you're fresh. Add distractions. When game day throws curveballs like bad turf, a hostile crowd, or terrible refs, your brain will not panic. Because you already trained for chaos.

Your limitations are not your enemy. They're your secret weapon. And the God who won battles with trumpets and clay jars is the same God standing with you right now. Whatever you don't have? That's just the space where His power moves in.

The Science Behind Limitation Training

Here's why this actually works inside your skull. Researcher Robert Bjork coined the term "desirable difficulties" in 1994. His studies showed that introducing strategic challenges into practice, making things intentionally harder, produces deeper and more durable learning than training under perfect conditions. When your environment is novel or uncomfortable, your brain releases norepinephrine and dopamine. Those are the neurochemicals responsible for focus, memory formation, and accelerated learning. Comfortable, familiar environments simply do not trigger these chemicals at the same level. Your brain literally learns FASTER when it's slightly stressed. Modern sports science calls this the "Constraints-Led Approach," and elite academies worldwide are now building entire training programs around it. Smaller tools, tighter spaces, rougher conditions. The science confirms what Giannis lived: limitation is not a punishment. It's premium brain fuel.

Prayer

Lord, help me stop wishing for perfect conditions and start thanking You for every limitation. Build Your strength in my weakness today. Amen.

Reflection: The Giannis Antetokounmpo Lesson

Giannis shared one pair of shoes with his brother and became a 2x NBA MVP and champion. His limitations did not limit him. They sharpened him. God's power showed up strongest where resources were weakest.

Ask yourself: What limitation in my life right now could actually be sharpening me into something stronger than I realize?

Mindset Drill: The 3-Minute Limitation Challenge (Every Practice Day)

This drill turns your "disadvantage" into your biggest edge. Do it before every training session.

» Minute 1: Choose ONE limitation for today's training. Pick from two categories. Tactical: use a smaller ball, practice with your weak hand or foot only, shrink the target to half its normal size, use half the court. Environmental:

practice outside instead of inside, do your skill work at the end of a workout when you're tired, add background noise or music, train on an imperfect surface. Write down which one you chose and why. Pen to paper. Make it real.

» Minute 2: Set a specific goal inside the limitation. Your brain needs a target to lock onto. Examples: "10 clean left-hand crossover moves using a tennis ball." "20 serves into a target half the normal size." "5 minutes of 3v3 with full communication every single possession." Do not just "practice hard." Give your brain a bullseye.

» Minute 3: Read 2 Corinthians 12:9 out loud. "My power is made perfect in weakness." Then pray this: "God, I'm training with less today so You can build more in me." Then go execute. Attack that limitation like Giannis attacked every cracked court in Athens.

Pro Tip: Keep a small "Limitation Log" in your notebook or phone. After each session, write what you limited and what you noticed. Within two weeks you will see patterns. Skills trained under constraint transfer to game day at a level that will genuinely shock you. Giannis built an empire from a pair of shared shoes. You can build one from a tennis ball and a half court.

Chapter Summary

Limitation sharpens you. Smaller tools build precision. Smaller spaces build speed. Rough environments activate brain chemicals that literally accelerate learning. Giannis Antetokounmpo shared shoes with his brother, trained on cracked courts, sold watches on the street, and became a 2x NBA MVP and NBA champion. Manny Pacquiao trained on dirt floors and became the greatest boxer of his generation. Playing small forces real teamwork where everyone matters and no one hides. God's power is made perfect in weakness. Stop wishing for better conditions. Embrace your limits and watch them become your deadliest advantage.

If You Want to Dive Deeper

To see how the "physics of adversity" applies to life outside the court, read the Autobiography of Theodore Roosevelt. He transformed childhood weakness into global leadership by intentionally seeking hardship to forge an indomitable will.

NOW IT'S YOUR TURN

"Therefore, my dear brothers and sisters, stand firm. Let nothing move you. Always give yourselves fully to the work of the Lord, because you know that your labor in the Lord is not in vain." — 1 Corinthians 15:58

You did it.

You actually finished this whole book. And let me tell you something real: most kids who pick up a book like this read the first chapter or two, nod a little, say "that's cool," and set it down on their nightstand where it collects dust next to an old water bottle and a half eaten granola bar. Not you. You went all the way through. Every chapter. Every drill. Every story. And that tells me something about you that no stat sheet, no ranking, and no coach's opinion ever could.

You're serious about becoming who God made you to be.

So before we close this thing out, let's walk through what you just built. Because this wasn't just a book you read. This was a training camp for your mind and your spirit. And you just completed every single session.

In Chapter 1, you met Steph Curry. The skinny kid from Charlotte that big colleges didn't even want. And Manny Pacquiao, the fourteen year old sleeping on cardboard in the Philippines with nothing but a huge decision burning in his heart. They both taught you the same thing: mental toughness starts with a decision, not a feeling. You don't sit around waiting until you feel brave. You decide first. You write your "I am" statement. You say it out loud every morning. And then your brain, your spirit, and eventually the whole world starts lining up with what you declared. Joshua 1:9 wasn't a polite suggestion. It was a command. Be courageous.

God's got your back.

In Chapter 2, Kevin Durant showed you what real humility looks like. This dude is basically seven feet tall with a trophy case full of scoring titles, and he STILL sat down and studied Dirk Nowitzki's fadeaway shot frame by frame. Still broke down Kobe's footwork like he was a student on the first day of school. Tyson Fury did the exact same thing, spending months studying Klitschko's fights before beating a champion everybody thought was unbeatable. They taught you the engraving technique: watch the greats with focused, locked in eyes. Let your brain download the blueprint. And they taught you to be careful about what you watch. Real game film builds real skills. Random trick shot videos on social media build fake confidence. Know the difference.

In Chapter 3, Tim Tebow walked you into the power of seeing it before it happens. Every football expert said he couldn't play quarterback at the pro level. Every scout picked apart his throwing motion. And then he threw an 80 yard overtime touchdown to shock the Pittsburgh Steelers in the playoffs. Why? Because he had already seen that moment in his mind a hundred times before it happened. He visualized with all five senses. He visualized with prayer. He didn't just picture things going perfectly. He also pictured things going wrong and saw himself bouncing back. That's Hebrews 11:1 with a helmet on. Faith is seeing what isn't there yet and believing it's already real. Your brain doesn't choke in moments it thinks it's already been through.

In Chapter 4, Serena Williams and her dad Richard showed you what happens when you write the vision down. Richard wrote a 78 page plan for Venus and Serena's tennis careers before they were even born. Goals on the walls. Dreams on paper. You learned the six rules of writing goals that actually stick, and you learned the obstacle upgrade, because real champions don't just dream about the finish line. They plan for the hard stuff that shows up along the way and write down exactly how they'll push through. God told the prophet Habakkuk to write the vision and make it plain. Not just think about it. Write it. So you did.

In Chapter 5, you went back to Manny Pacquiao. But this time you weren't watching him fight. You were watching him between rounds. Eyes closed. Breathing slowly. Praying. Standing across from men who wanted to knock him out cold, and looking completely peaceful. You learned that your breath is the only thing in your body you can control on purpose AND that runs on its own. That makes it like a remote control for your whole nervous system. Box breathing calms you down in 60 seconds. Navy SEALs use it when bullets are flying. The physiological sigh resets you in one single breath. You can use it between plays, before free throws, between pitches, anytime pressure hits. Genesis 2:7 says the very first gift God ever gave humans was a breath. That breath has more power than you ever knew.

In Chapter 6, Usain Bolt taught you that the fastest person alive was also the most relaxed. While every other sprinter in the Olympic final looked tight and stressed, Bolt was dancing and smiling. Not because he didn't care. Because his mind was quiet, and a quiet mind lets your body do what it was trained to do. You learned that meditation opens the door to the zone, and slow practice builds the clean pathways in your brain that your speed will eventually ride on. You learned that a slump isn't you losing your talent. It's a little glitch in your brain's wiring that you fix by slowing down, going back to basics, and rebuilding. Psalm 46:10 says be still. Not be busy. Not be faster. Be still. And in that stillness, God builds something amazing.

In Chapter 7, Giannis Antetokounmpo showed you that starting with nothing can actually be your greatest advantage. Sharing one pair of shoes with his brother. Selling stuff on the streets of Athens just to eat. Playing on cracked outdoor courts with terrible equipment. And then becoming a two time MVP and NBA champion. You learned that training with less builds more. Smaller tools sharpen your hands. Tighter spaces speed up your brain. Rough conditions make you tougher than any fancy gym ever could. And 2 Corinthians 12:9 confirmed what Giannis lived out every single day: God's power shows up strongest when you feel weakest.

Seven chapters. Seven drills. Seven athletes who walked through fire and came out the other side wearing gold. And now those same tools live inside YOU.

But here's the part I need to be straight with you about.

Knowing these drills and actually doing them are two totally different things. It's like watching basketball highlights all day but never going outside to shoot. The highlights don't make you better. The reps do. These drills have to leave these pages and enter your mornings, your practices, your game days, and your real life.

Start tomorrow. Not next week. Not "when the new season starts." Tomorrow morning. Do the Decision Declaration from Chapter 1. Three minutes. Out loud. Then add one new drill every few days until you've stacked all seven. Twenty one minutes a day. That's shorter than one episode of whatever show you're watching right now. And it will change everything about how you compete and how you live.

In 30 days you'll feel different. In one season you'll carry yourself different. And over a lifetime? You'll become the kind of person other people look up to and say, "I want to be like that."

Because here's the final truth, and I want this one to stick with you forever: the discipline, courage, honesty, toughness, focus, and faith you built in these pages? Those aren't just sports skills. Those are life skills. Most athletes won't go pro one day. That's just how the numbers work. But every single athlete will face moments that demand real mental toughness and real character. A test that feels impossible. A friendship that falls apart. A dream that seems way too big. A moment where quitting sounds easier than pushing forward. When those moments come, and trust me they will, you won't just have talent. You'll have something deeper. Something trained into your mind and planted in your spirit.

You were not built to be average. You were called to be a champion. Not just in your sport. In your home. In your friendships. In your faith. In everything God has planned for you that you can't even see yet.

One more thing before you go.

Think about someone you know. A teammate. A friend. A brother or sister. Someone who plays sports and loves competing but maybe struggles with confidence, or gets in their own head, or doesn't know how strong they really are. Share this book with them. Better yet, read it together. Do the drills together. Hold each other accountable. Push each other. Because champions don't rise alone. They rise as a team. And the best thing you can do with something that changed you is pass it on to someone you care about.

Stand firm. Let nothing move you. Be UNSHAKABLE.

If you loved these athlete stories and want to read even more true stories of sports heroes whose faith carried them through every trial, pick up Called to Be a Champion. It's full of powerful, real stories of athletes who walked with God through the toughest moments of their careers and came out stronger on the other side. It's the perfect next book for your UNSHAKABLE journey.

A TRUE BLESSING!

If this book has encouraged you or helped you feel less alone, would you leave a quick review?

Even one sentence makes a huge difference and takes just a minute. As a small author, your feedback not only lifts my heart... it also helps other women of faith with find the support and hope they need.

Thank you for being part of this journey!

Scan this QR code with your phone to go to the review page and find this book.

Or

Go to your orders, find the book and click

"Write a product review"

Thank you <3